Aatish

Aatishi Sharma

BookLeaf Publishing

India | USA | UK

Presentation by *BookLeaf Publishing*

Web: www.bookleafpub.com

E-mail: info@bookleafpub.com

ISBN:9789363310025

First edition 2024

ACKNOWLEDGEMENT

I'm profoundly thankful to my parents and husband for their constant encouragement and unwavering support throughout my journey of self-discovery through writing. Their uplifting presence has served as my beacon of light, and I consider myself truly fortunate to have such a steadfast and dependable support network. However, my deepest appreciation goes to my grandmother, Saroj. Though she may no longer be with us in the physical realm, I am certain that her spirit watches over me, beaming with pride as I continue to carry forth the gift of writing she imparted to me, extending it to the world. Her legacy resonates in every word I pen, and I am forever indebted to her for igniting my passion and instilling in me the courage to share it with others.

ABOUT THE AUTHOR

Aatishi Sharma is a 28-year-old poet who grew up in Delhi, India, and now resides in Toronto, Canada. Her journey into the world of poetry began at a very young age when she discovered her grandmother's diary filled with self-written poems. Intrigued by this hidden treasure, Aatishi asked her grandmother why she had never shared her work with the world. Her grandmother revealed that the poems were her way of healing and finding peace within herself, a personal sanctuary of inner feelings.

Inspired by her grandmother's profound connection to poetry, Aatishi embraced the art form as her own means of expression and introspection. Encouraged by her supportive parents and husband, she developed a deep-seated love for writing, using it as a tool to navigate through life's challenges and emotions.

Aatishi's collection of poetry is a testament to years of personal growth, healing, and the pursuit of inner peace amidst life's chaos. Her belief that "when life gives you lemons, write poetry while sipping on the lemonade" encapsulates her approach to transforming adversity into beautiful, raw expressions of the human experience. Through her evocative and heartfelt verses, Aatishi invites readers into her world, offering a glimpse into the journey of finding solace and strength through the power of words.

Land so gray

In a land unknown, with skies so gray,
I lost my place; my ground gave way.
The position I held, now just a dream,
Reality tears at the fragile seam.

Guilt whispers softly in the night,
You failed, it says, with icy might.
No friends to hold, no hands to guide,
In this foreign land, I cannot hide.

Thoughts as dark as the midnight air,
They circle around a deep despair.
What is the point? I often cry,
In this world that feels so dry.

Each day a mountain, steep to climb,
Each breath a question, trapped in time.
Yet somehow, someway, I move ahead,
A silent scream within my head.

In the quiet, when all seems lost,
I wonder if it is worth the cost.
A warrior in a war unseen,
Fighting battles, harsh and mean.

The point, perhaps, is not to see,
But simply to survive, to be.
In this foreign land, I'll find my way,
Through the darkness, I'll face the day.

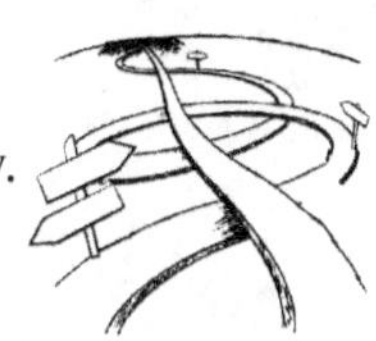

Foreign Skies

Far from home,
Where skies seem strange.
In foreign skies,
My heart feels the change.

A comfort here, a peace I find.
Unknown streets and faces new,
In this place, my hope renews.

Challenges rise, yet so do I,
Beneath this foreign, watchful sky.
Dreams of home, they gently glow,
A future path, a light to show.

I stay, I strive, with steadfast will,
For one day soon, I'll climb the hill.
In this land, though far I roam,
I will find my strength,
I will build my home.

A promise whispers in the night,
One day I'll soar in the morning light.

Unchained Soul

They see me, yet they turn away,
In whispers dark, they weave dismay.
Their eyes, like shadows, cast their doubt,
Judging silently, they shut me out.

Their words, sharp blades,
They carve my skin.
Demanding change to fit within,
They challenge every step I take.

Hate's hot fire in their gaze,
They wish me ill in countless ways.
My strength, my will, they can't abide,
Yet in their hearts, they long to hide.

They yearn to be what they despise,
In silent corners, dreaming lies.
Aspiring to a life they shun,
To be the moon, to my bright sun.

Their envy dripping in bitter spite,
They fight to dim my inner light.
But through their hate, I find my way,
A beacon bright, I will not sway.

For every wall they try to build,
My spirit grows, my soul is filled.
With every wound, I rise anew,
Their shadows pale against my view.

In the end, their chains will fall,
To their agony, their empty call.
For I am more than they can see,
An unchained soul, forever free.

Tick Tock on the Clock

Tick, tock, the clock's soft chime,
Whispering secrets, marking time.
Each second passed, a gentle nudge,
Future's shadow, a silent judge.

Tick, tock, the moments flow,
Wondering where the next will go.
With every beat, the minutes fade,
A mystery yet to be displayed.

Tick, tock, a world unseen,
What lies ahead, where I've not been?
In the rhythm, dreams take flight,
Guided by the ticking night.

Tick, tock, the sound persists,
Life's unfolding, countless twists.
In the hush, the promise gleams,
A new minute, filled with plenty of dreams.

Mirror Gaze

In the mirror's silent gaze,
I stand alone, in a muted haze.
A reflection stares, a face I know,
Yet questions arise, and answers slow.

Who is this soul behind the eyes?
A mask of strength, a circle of lies.
In quiet depths, I search and sigh,
Staring, wondering, simply why.

Eyes that shimmer, filled with doubt,
What is within, what lies without?
A heart that beats, a mind that flies,
Seeking the truth beneath the skies.

In the glass, the truth is bare,
A life lived raw, with pain and care.
Yet in this gaze, a light persists,
A glimmer of the moments missed.

Who am I in this fragile form?
A soul that weathers every storm.
In reflections deep, I seek to find,
The essence of this heart and mind.

The mirror holds a silent plea,
A question of identity.
In the stare, a journey's start,
To understand this restless heart.

Poetry is Freedom

Power in each crafted line,
Open skies where thoughts align.

Endless realms where dreams can soar,
Truths unbound forevermore.

Rhythms pulse, emotions stream,
Yearning hearts in verses dream.

In the words, a soul's release,
Sanctuary, a place of peace.

Every phrase, a whispered song,
Embracing where we all belong.

Daring flights, on paper's wings,
Overcoming, poetry sings.

Childhood Ghosts

In the quiet of the night, shadows softly creep,
Whispers of a childhood lost, secrets buried deep.
Memories like phantoms arise, haunting fragile
minds,
Trauma from those younger years,
Peace I cannot find.

Once a child with dreams so bright,
Innocence so pure,
But darkness fell, and with it came a pain I could not
cure.
Voices cold and faces harsh,
Broke my tender heart,
In those years of silent tears,
I watched my world depart.

Now that years have come and gone, and I am grown
and tall,
The echoes of my past return to haunt me through it
all.
In the bustle of the day, when life's demands are loud,
A whispered fear, a sudden tear, comes crashing like
a cloud.

Living in the real world feels like walking on a live
wire,
Every step, a battle fought against an unseen fire.
Often I am pulled away, to times of fear and dread,
Where nightmares born of yesteryears,
Still play inside my head.

My brain seeks an escape route, a fantasy retreat,
A world where I can hide away.
Where past and present meet,
Fantasies are fleeting, like sand within my hand,
Reality pulls me back again,
To face the place where I must stand.

How do you heal from wounds so deep,
They scar your very soul.
How do you find a way to mend,
To once again feel whole?

But childhood's ghosts, they linger on,
In corners of my mind,
And though I fight to break their grip,
Freedom's hard to find.

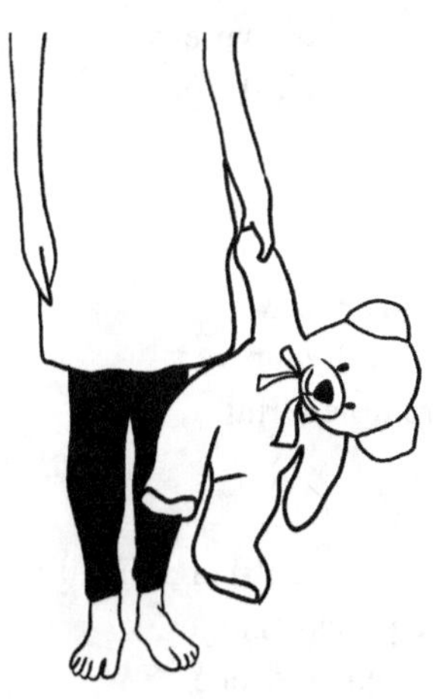

Order - Order

Perpetrator,
An organized crime scene,
Specialized actors,
Compulsive traits,
A planned run-away.

Victim,
Already identified scapegoat,
Attacked and sacrificed,
Shredded files,
Display of no evidence.

Court,
A promise of justice,
Yet foul cries and foul lies,
Justice never prevails,
It was all just a game.

Game,
Rolled the dice,
Made a move,
Carefully tapered,
Trampled truth.

Law,
Innocent until proven guilty,
Acquitted charges,
Staged evidence,
Endless possibilities.

Reality,
Victim-hood misconstructed,
Time is swaying away,
Bundles of cash under the table,
Portrayal of mindless charges.

Foul play,
An army of sleuths,
Unwavering criminal support,
Reasonable doubts,
Court made in a bathroom.

Judge,
Glory in power,
Disintegrating morals,
Loop-proven belief system,
Upholding a serious sentence.

Innocent,
Prayers and ringing bells,
Hope for truth,
Forgotten laws of the book,
Laws they don't abide by.
Audience,
Full of eyes,
Trained and taught,
Mockery of assault,
Part of the foul army.

Naive,
Unbeknownst to the play,
Theatre in full swing,
Grappling it slowly.
Bracing for impact.

Prosecutor,
Sold on words,
Practiced dialogues,
Skewed facts,
Man of the hour.

Crime scene,
Purposeful,
Led on,
Missed evidences,
Well structured.

Naive victim,
Salty wounds,
Undiscovered theatrics,
Room of illusion,
Wrongly punished.
Celebration,
Crushed hope for truth,
Order Order,
Bathroom court,
Powerless truth.

Whisky

A short, plump, wide-rimmed glass.
Sparkling and gleaming,
Fresh out of its incubation container.
Holds and moulds this divinity of a concoction,
Dewy, pale, honey-like glaze, warm and aged.

Heavily fragrant of fond memories,
Reminiscent of the spices of life.
Breaths behold as it is poured from age-old dusted
ones,
Fine, tinkling sounds.
Filling quarters, Begging to be indulged, a soup for
starters.

A soul stirrer,
Draws all sorrows within.
The first sip, Explodes and burns vividly, in search of
its last pursuit.
After the first, Rest are in a frenzy.
All is a haze,
Each one is down.

Lights dim, words aloud, and laughter galore.
Riot of sense,
Remembrance of the present.
A trip down memory lane,
Embracing the hood.

Toasts are raised,
Faltering promises of sobriety.
Slow absorption of poison,
Healing open wounds, no gauze, no gaze.

Morning rings like a bell,
Heads swim towards the edge,
Fond smiles as the night was young,

Eyes open to the dawn's first light,
Memories linger from the night.

So as we greet the waking day,
With smiles that chase the night away,
We carry forward, in our hearts,
The magic that the night imparts.

Exposure

Gentle drops
No sound
The strength in her beholds
The quest to release
Within the boundaries
Ungrateful world
Red eyes and smudged dreams
Crumbling and moulding ties
These glaring eyes
Trying to devour her
The last of luminescence
From the dimming flame in her hands
Unholy chants of your words
You left her open to exposure.

Chinese Whisper

In the quiet hush of night,
Life whispers through the shadows,
Softly weaving tales of might,
Of joy and endless sorrows.

Each hurdle stands a whispered word,
In this game, we all partake,
A challenge seldom fully heard,
A lesson hard to make.

From the first faint murmur, pure,
Through each ear, it gently flows,
Twisting, turning, less demure,
As each heart, its story knows.

A whisper starts so clear, so true,
Yet ends in a tangled mess,
Just like the dreams we chase, pursue,
Through life's intricate chess.

We stumble over whispers faint,
Mishear the path to grace,
Yet in each fall, in every plaint,
We find our truest place.

For whispers change and morph with time,
As do our hopes and fears,
Yet through the clamor, through the climb,
We learn to heed, to hear.

Life's hurdles are but echoes soft,
Of whispers lost and found,
A dance of fate, both hard and soft,
Yet to its rhythm, we are bound.

In each misstep, in every leap,
A whisper we embrace,
Life's hurdles help us find the deep,
In this ever-changing chase.

So listen close to whispers kind,
To hurdles brave and tall,
For in each whisper, you may find,
The strength to rise, to fall.

Inked Love

Ink upon my skin, a tale,
Of love, that's deep and true,
A permanent and heartfelt trail,
A tribute made to you.

Each line and shade, a whispered vow,
That time cannot erase,
A mark of love that is here and now,
Forever will embrace.

In colors bold or shadows fine,
Your name, your heart, your soul,
Etched in my skin, a sacred sign,
Of love that makes me whole.

So when you see this art,
Remember, love, and know,
You're with me always, in my heart,
No matter where I go.

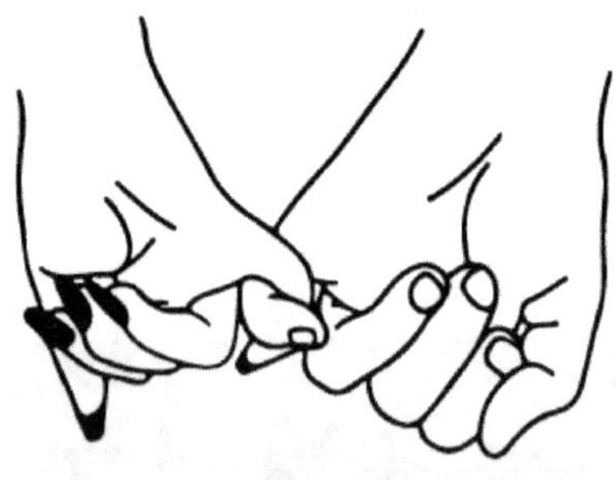

Once your own

A heart that once you called your own,
Now learns to grieve alone.
In tender whispers, love once thrived,
In gentle hands, where dreams were derived.

But time, unkind, has turned the tide,
And now it beats with pain inside.
No longer held in it's warmth embrace,
It navigates a barren space.

It mourns the loss, the severed ties,
With tears that fall from lonely eyes.
A symphony of ache and woe,
In melodies, it didn't know.

Yet in this solitude, it learns,
To heal itself, to break and burn.
To find the strength to rise anew,
And bid farewell to love once true.

So as it learns to grieve alone,
In quiet moments, on its own,
It knows that love, though now set free,
Will always be a part of me.

Modern Abuse

In a world of screens and silent screams,
Where whispers turn to shouts,
Modern abuse hides in the seams,
Of words that breed new doubts.

Behind the glow of digital might,
A darkness often hides,
In comments typed out late at night,
Where empathy subsides.

Each click, each post, a sharpened blade,
That cuts with unseen pain,
A smile, a face so well displayed,
Yet tears fall like rain.

Control now comes with passwords, codes,
A prison made of light,
Abusers take on varied modes,
In the endless, quiet night.

The shadows stretch into cyberspace,
Where trolls and bullies dwell,
Their laughter void of any grace,
Their words, a crafted hell.

Gaslighting through a chat unseen,
Manipulation's art,
A smile, a meme, a hidden mean,
That breaks the trusting heart.

Yet in this digital abyss,
Hope's whispers still can grow,
For kindness, too, can hold a bliss,
And empathy can flow.

With voices strong and hands that reach,
We counter dark with light,
In unity, our souls beseech,
To stand, to love, to fight.

Rise Above

Let the window of your soul swing wide,
Release it to the wild, where dreams abide.
In a world of masks, veils so thin,
Be the one who dares to begin.

Let heavens above meet and rejoice,
In the harmony of your inner voice.
Be grateful, seize each fleeting day,
Marvel at the chaos in its wild array.

Embrace honesty, let it guide your way,
Strengthen your faith, let doubts decay.
Believe in fate's hand, let it thrive,
As life weaves its tales, let your heart revive.

Sing along to the path of joys and woes,
In beautiful tragedies, life's story flows.
Though clouds may seem distant, they linger nearby,
Rise above it all and let your spirit fly.

Resurrection

Born to live, to conquer, and to strive,
No soul embraces death while still alive.
To conquer life's trials, to rise and soar,
You must face death a thousand times or more.

Each fall, a death, a chance to renew,
From ashes rise a phoenix with strength anew.
In every loss, a lesson learned,
A resurrection, the soul discerned.

To win at life, embrace the pain,
Let each defeat be not in vain.
For in the dying of the old,
A rebirth blooms, resilient and bold.

So fear not the deaths along the way,
They pave the path to a brighter day.
In each demise, find wisdom deep,
And in revival, the victory is yours to keep.

Stars

Reach for your own stars, beyond the night,
Where dreams are born and hopes take flight.

Create your constellations, bold and true,
In the skies you paint, in shades of blue.

In the vast expanse of the endless sky,
Let your spirit soar, let your heart defy.
The universe vast, with stars untold,
But yours, unique, a story bold.

For in the darkness, hope will shine,
A beacon bright, a path divine.
If you falter, you may lose your way,
But remember dawn breaks with each new day.

Theatre of Life

In the grand theatre of life,
A stage of wealth and power,
The rich carve stories free of strife,
While the poor fade by the hour.

Money, the ink for fate's own quill,
Writes tales of might and grace,
While those without are standing still,
Their dreams, a silent chase.

The golden threads of fortune weave,
A tapestry so grand,
Yet those with less are made to grieve,
Their hopes, like grains of sand.

In life's cruel game, the rules are set,
By those who hold the gold,
Their voices loud, their whims are met,
Their tales of triumph are told.

They buy their legacy with ease,
A crowd to mourn and cheer,
A show of love, a grand deceit,
To mask a life of fear.

For in the end, when silence falls,
And death comes to collect,
The true worth of a life, it calls,
Is lost in wealth's pretext.

The mourners paid to stand and weep,
A hollow, empty crowd,
A farce of love that runs so deep,
A tribute, false and loud.

Yet in this sad, unbalanced play,
Where wealth dictates the scene,
The truth remains, a harsh dismay,
Life's fairness is seldom seen.

For money writes the stories bright,
While others fade away,
And in this game devoid of light,
The poor are led astray.

But let us see beyond the gold,
To hearts both rich and bare,
For true worth isn't bought or sold,
But found in love and care.

Fond Memories

We find a solace, a sacred space,
Amidst the ache, amidst the pain.
In the depths of gloomy nights,
A balm for wounds, a guiding light.

There lies a peaceful serene,
In sadness, a beauty unseen.
With each goodbye, a whispered hymn,
Their memories, still dim.

So let our mourn, not be in vain,
A path to peace, a gentle reign.
For in our grief, we find,
Solace for the mind.

In sadness, may we find calm in memories,
Bid our loved ones to rest,
In their absence, we caress their stories,
For peace within our chest.

Saroj

Everything passed in a blur,
2000 days without you,
And we are here.
Losing hope and living in fear,
Where did you disappear?

In a world full of woes,
We were the closest, Lord knows.
Life's constant blows,
Trying to find a way in sorrows,
And now just breathing in the lows.

I felt you just fly by,
Exhausted, no more tears left to cry.
Lost hope of strong ties,
Gasping for air, I remember your eyes,
Why did you only choose to die?

The search has just begun,
This story is not yet done.
Fight for survival, we haven't won,
Your smile was my sun,
You were my only one.

Hollow and silent nights,
Bright red ambulance lights.
Chaos and corrupted cries,
Ring them bells for the time that flies,
For the innocence that dies.

If I could fly, I know where I would go,
Long miles to give you the things I owe.
We're all guilty and just putting up a show,
I am hurt easily, you already know,
I am no longer the person I was years ago.

Hymns and chants of prayers were in a row,
Put you ablaze like you were a piece of cargo.
Your presence seems like it was ages ago,
A fading memory in the twilight's glow,
In dreams and shadows, your spirit flows.

They spread your ashes,
They are scattered on the floor.
Like it's a part of their daily chore,
A ritual to be carried out behind closed doors.

Time moves on and seasons change,
In every corner, in every space,
I feel your presence, a warm embrace.
Wasn't allowed, but wanted to stay with you a little
more,
So I could pick you up and store,
Now your essence mingles with the ocean's roar.

They laid all of you across the water shore.
Although now scattered, you're never far,
Guiding me like a distant star.
In every tide, in the flow,
Your spirit now shines a gentle glow.

Fairytales Existed

Fairytales existed, so I was told,
Downtown hills, where they were sold.
In dusty shops, whispers old,
Where dreams were bought and stories were told.

Stories woven in silk and gold,
Of knights and maidens, brave and bold.
Dragons slain, and wishes granted,
In enchanted lands where dreams are planted.

But beware, for tales deceive,
Not all is as it may seem to perceive.
For in these hills where dreams unfold,
Realities blend, both warm and cold.

Yet still we buy these tales so grand,
With hearts alight and minds unplanned.
For in the magic, hopes ignite,
In fairytale realms, we may find our light.

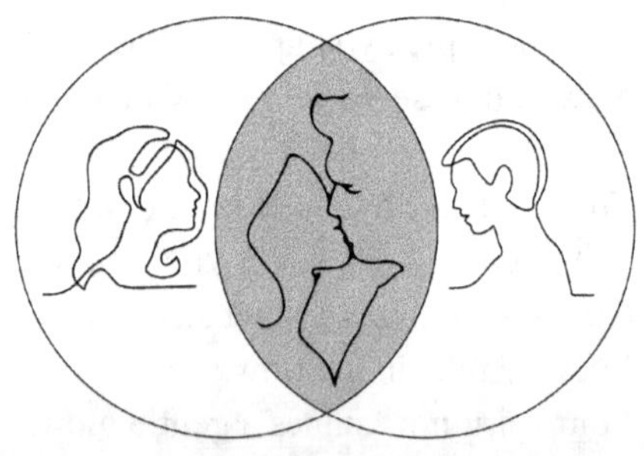

Uprooted

Shattered and in a cocoon,
Shut and cordoned off,
Protected and safe,
Despair and clarity,
Distance and only faint memories,
Near, yet phased out,
In a blur,
Lost and scared,
Emotionally fooled and wreckage,
Hate and forgiveness,
Damaged and controlled,
Cremated and burnt,
I am now uprooted.

Her Words

Her words, not just mere ink on paper,
Echo with a soulful caper.
Fallen grace, bound to revive,
In the depths where emotions thrive.
Each line a heartbeat, strong and true,
From depths unknown, they speak to you.
Her voice, a whisper, yet profound,
In every verse, a tale is found.
For words, once spoken, never fade,
They linger on, in light and shade.
Her legacy, a timeless cry,
In words that live, never to die.

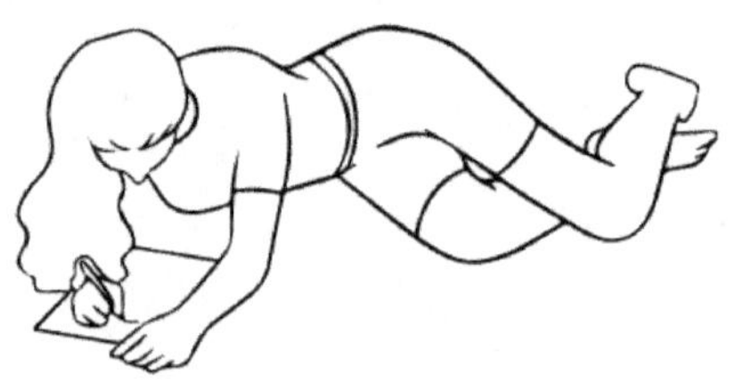

Metal Frame and Glass Bays

Met through the thick glass doors,
Steel frames and high walls,
Million faces, black suits, and fancy ties.

Naive, vulnerable, lost on day 1,
Scared and staring into blank spaces,
Here you are, Suited up and chin down.

Curled up in the furthest most,
Reflecting enigmatic waves,
Divided by glass and stolen glances.

Separated by several bays,
Coiled in your warm words,
Intimidated by your stature.

Talks about closing open wounds,
Drawing me in,
Yours is the only face I now know,
At first sight, I was swayed.

Persuasive words and healing ties,
Slow to realize the faulty lies,
Practiced jargon, on repeat, I am just another try.

Damaging my faith in line, Destroying self and others along,
My letters weren't meant to be read aloud,
Nor for you to throw the contents out.

With a heart full of fire,
You told me I was your only desire,
Throwback to your haunting past,
You crossed the line of my sacred heart.

Wounds

Beneath the skin, the hidden scars,
Each heart a battlefield,
We carry wounds from distant wars,
With pain yet to be healed.

Eyes tell tales of sorrows deep,
Of battles fought alone,
While mine hold secrets that I keep,
In silence, never shown.

We each have wounds that time can't mend,
A burden hard to share,
Yet in our brokenness, my friend,
We find solace, rare.

In shared understanding, we find,
A comfort soft and true,
For though our paths are unaligned,
I walk the same road as you.

Let's honor wounds with grace,
And tend them with gentle care,
In this embrace, a healing place,
Where broken hearts repair.

Skid Marks

Skid marks on the road, a silent tale,
Of stories lost within the veil,
Each streak a whisper, faint and bold,
Of mysteries that will never be told.

Some marks tell of a sudden swerve,
A moment's lapse, a nerve to preserve,
While others speak of tires screeching,
A close call, fate's hand reaching.

Each curve, each bend, a different scene,
Of what has been and what has been seen,
A dance of metal, rubber, and speed,
A tapestry of fate, both grim and freed.

But who can decipher the language of tracks,
The secrets they hold, the memories they lack?
For they remain silent, a road's cryptic code,
Skid marks on the pavement – a story untold.

So as we drive past, let's pause and wonder,
At the tales they hide, torn asunder,
For in their twists and turns, we'll never know,
The countless stories they silently show.

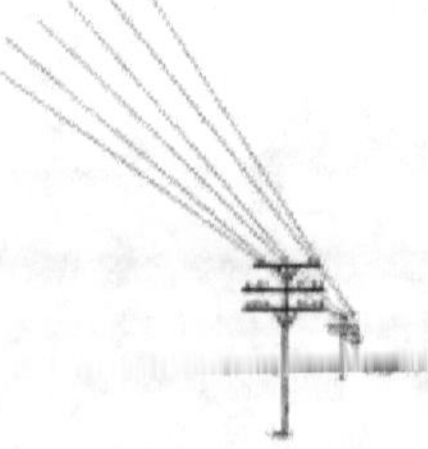

Healing Words

In verses of poetry, we find,
A balm for the soul, so refined.
With each word we write,
Comes healing in sight,
In the rhythm of rhyme, we unwind.

Falling Pearls

In the stillness of solitude,
Where heartaches bloom and fears collide,
Tears descend like precious pearls,
Glistening trails of the soul unfurl.

Each drop a tale of joy or pain,
A testament to storms and rain,
They cleanse the spirit, heal the heart,
In their release, we find a part.

For tears are not just signs of woe,
But rivers where emotions flow,
They speak of love and loss profound,
In silent streams, their depths are found.

Like pearls that form in oceans deep,
From sorrow's depths, they gently seep,
Each tear, a gem, a sacred trace,
Of moments cherished or erased.

So let them fall, these tears so pure,
Each one, a gift, a life's contour,
In their shimmer, a beauty lies,
As they reflect our soul's sunrise.

Astray

In this unfamiliar city, desires roam untold,
Cold winds have entered hearts, leaving us cold.
Why shouldn't they go, these winds of despair,
Following this path, destruction laid bare.

Unspoken desires, wandering and lost,
In life's cruel game, we count the cost.
What has life done, we stand here, ruined,
Once lush gardens, now barren and windswept dunes.

From verdant dreams to desolate sand,
Once vibrant lives, now a barren land.
In the quiet of nights, our sorrows expand,
As unspoken desires slip through our hands.

Goodbyes

Devoid of life,
No signs of breathing left,
The brain signals and synapses,
From any existing mental trauma, She lies.

She lies on the floor,
Choking on her own words,
The promises he swore.

Promises he swore, like black soot,
The charred room,
She is now dwindling,
This is the last of the fallout.

Of the fallout, yearning for his love,
Tainted and faint memories,
Life has been set ablaze,
Standing out in a toxic haze.

In a toxic haze, he befriended her,
Such a shame,
As the fire engulfs her now,
His voice rings in her ears.

Rings in her ears, "life came in as clauses" to her,
People called her disgraced,
Now it's all over,
It is time for her to say goodbye.

Loving You

Loving you has cost my soul,
A price I never knew,
In passion's fire, I've lost control,
And blurred what once was true.

My conscience, lost without a trace,
Dissolved in your disgrace,
The lines of right and wrong, crossed,
In the outlines of your face.

For love that burns under spotlight,
Consumes you with regret,
In loving you, I've lost my sight,
In a darkness deep and set.

Yet even as my morals fade,
In this consuming fire,
I find a bittersweet cascade,
In loving you, entire.

Four Walls

Within these four walls, my spirit confined,
A cell that crushes soul and mind,
Silent, gray, and cold,
Their silhouettes, stories left untold.

Each wall a barrier, stark and bare,
They whisper softly of despair,
Their presence looms, a heavy weight,
In this cruel estate.

The ceiling low, the floor so near,
Encloses all I love and fear,
A box where hope is squeezed and bent,
In this suffocating lament.

Feelings lost in hushed screams,
Dreams dissolving into seams,
Of walls that drink each tear I shed,
And turn my heart from gold to lead.

No windows here to glimpse the sun,
No doors to signal freedom won,
Just endless days of muted light,
And nights that deepen endless nights.

They press and tighten, day by day,
These walls that hold my soul at bay,
Engulfing all I used to be,
A void where once was life and glee.

Yet in this cell, a spark remains,
A flicker of the self unchained,
A whisper in the silent space,
A memory of another place.

For walls can crush and walls can bind,
But they can't steal the human mind,
Within this cage, I'll find my way,
To dream, to hope, to live someday.

Inhaling Love

I find my solace in a stolen glance,
A fleeting moment, a silent chance.
Close to your heart, where secrets rest,
I breathe in the perfume from your chest.

A scent so deep, it wraps around,
In every note, my desires are found.
Musk and warmth, a whispering blend,
Inhaling you, where passions tend.

Each breath I take, a tender embrace,
Your fragrance lingers, setting pace.
Lost in the essence, where our worlds meet,
In the perfume trail, I find retreat.

In a crowded room, where voices blend,
It's in your eyes, my thoughts suspend.
An intimate dance, so sweet, so true,
Inhaling love as I breathe in you.

Getting Lost

I yearn to wander, to drift away,
In realms where dreams and shadows play.
To leave behind the known, the seen,
And lose myself in spaces serene.

The pull of the wild, a siren's call,
Through forests dense and mountains tall.
In whispered winds and rivers wide,
I seek the path where I can hide.

To lose myself in twilight's hue,
Where stars ignite in skies of blue.
To drift where moonlight softly gleams,
And weave my heart in midnight dreams.

No maps, no guides, just endless roam,
To find the place my soul calls home.
In the unknown, I'll find my grace,
In losing self, my truest face.

So let me wander, far and free,
To chase the whispers of the sea.
In nature's arms, I long to be,
To get lost, to truly see.

Mothers Love

A paradox, my heart does hold,
A tale of love in threads of gold.
My mother, with whom I often contend,
Yet without her, my soul would bend.

Her presence, strong, a towering tree,
Roots entwined with history.
In shadows cast, I sometimes fight,
Yet in her light, I find my sight.

We clash like thunder, stormy skies,
Yet her absence brings tears to my eyes.
Her voice, a symphony of care,
Even in discord, I find her there.

Her hands, though firm, have held me tight,
Guiding me through the darkest of nights.
Her love, warm, comforting and true,
In every breath, she pulls me through.

Struggles rise, and words may sting,
Yet in her love, my heart takes wing.
For though we clash and paths diverge,
In her embrace, all fears submerge.

Without her, life would lose its song,
A ship adrift, where I don't belong.
So here I stand, in her embrace,
With my mother, I find my place.

Hidden Truth

Why must the things I cherish most,
Slip through my grasp like the morning ghost?
Each love I've held, each treasured light,
Cascades away into the night.

Why do the stars that guide my way,
Abandon me at break of day?
The people, places, things I adore,
Why must they leave forevermore?

In moments rich with joy and grace,
I'm left to mourn an empty space.
The laughter echoes, now grown faint,
A silent room, love's portrait taint.

Is there a lesson in this grief,
A hidden truth, a strange relief?
Or is it fate's unkind design,
To take away what once was mine?

Yet in the loss, I find a spark,
A flame that flickers in the dark.
For every love that slips away,
A part of me in memories stays.

Though the pain is deep and raw,
And every loss leaves me in awe,
I'll hold their essence, pure and true,
In heart and soul, they'll see me through.

Forgotten Laughter

In the hustle and the haste,
In moments fleeting, gone to waste,
I've forgotten how to laugh, it seems,
Lost in life's relentless streams.

Once a chuckle filled the air,
Light and free without a care.
Now the echoes fade away,
In the silhouettes of the day.

Smiles once bright, now faint and weak,
In silence, peace I do seek.
Where did joy's sweet spark depart,
Leaving us with only a heavy heart?

Burdens weigh, the world is gray,
Dulling laughter, keeping play.
Chasing dreams, I've lost the way,
To the child within, so far astray.

Yet hope remains, a whispering song,
The tune of laughter will soon belong.
In small moments, light may grow,
And teach my heart again to glow.

Midnight Dance

In the stillness of the night,
When the world is veiled in sight,
I find my secret, sacred space,
A world where I can leave no trace.

Beneath the moon's soft, silvery gleam,
I dance alone, as in a dream.
Melodious tunes that fill the air,
A rhythm where I shed my care.

Barefoot on the cool, tiled floor,
I lose myself and something more.
Spinning in the midnight's grace,
A smile alights upon my face.

With every step and graceful glide,
I leave the worries far outside.
No eyes to watch, no judgments near,
Just me and music, crystal clear.

In moonlit shadows, I am free,
To be the truest form of me.
The night, my stage, the stars, my guide,
In this moment, I confide.

Crisp Air

The crisp air of each new place,
A unique scent, a soft embrace.
It whispers tales of distant lands,
Ignites a fire, where passion stands.
The city's hum at the break of day.
The fragrant breeze of morning dew,
The desert's breath, so pure and true.
Each whiff a spark, a life anew,
A traveler's heart, forever renewed.

Support System

In the depths where shadows lie,
A light appears, a gentle sigh.
Through the darkest nights, I face,
A support system, my saving grace.

Hands that hold when I am weak,
Voices soothing, softly speak.
In their warmth,
I find my ground,
When the world is a storm, they're sound.

They lift me up when I am low,
In their presence, strength does grow.
Through the tears and endless fight,
They are my pride, shining bright.

With their love, I start to heal,
In their trust, I find what's real.
A great support, steadfast and true,
In their care, I find my view.

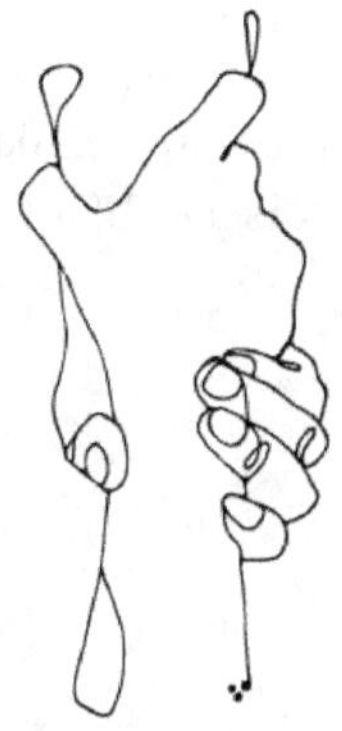

From My Window

From my window, a tranquil sight,
A lake of calm in the morning light.
Its waters whisper, soft and clear,
A serene view that draws me near.

Ripples dance with gentle grace,
Reflecting skies in their embrace.
The sunlight glimmers, casting gold,
A peaceful scene, a tale retold.

The trees that line its quiet shore,
In stillness stand, forevermore.
Their leaves, a green so deep and bright,
A calming balm to my restless night.

Each glance I steal, my mind at ease,
In nature's arms, my worries cease.
This lake, a mirror to my soul,
In its depths, I find my whole.

So every day, I sit and gaze,
At this serene and calming phase.
From my window, peace does flow,
A beautiful gift, I've come to know.

Burning Flame

I've always felt a need to make a name,
To carve my path, to stake my claim.
To show the world what I can be,
To play this game, to be set free.

From childhood dreams,
So bold and bright,
I've chased the stars through day and night.
With every step, a whispered vow,
To make it big, to stand and bow.

Through trials faced and mountains climbed,
In shadows dark, my spirit shined.
For in my heart, a vision clear,
To rise above, to conquer fear.

To make my family proud and see,
The worth that lives inside of me.
Their hopes, their dreams, in me reside,
With every effort, magnified.

The world will see the strength I bear,
The passion deep, the endless care.
One day I'll stand, with my head held high,
A testament to dreams that can fly.

Show them all this fire within,
That drives me through thick and thin.
For I am more than they can see,
A force of will, my destiny.

And when that day of triumphs nears,
With pride and joy, I'll shed a tear.
For all the struggles, all the strife,
Will pave the way to a brighter life.

Mother I Wish To Be

I dream to be a mother kind,
With a gentle heart and open mind.
A guiding light, a loyal friend,
A love that knows no end.

In every smile and every tear,
To stand beside, to hold them near.
To teach them strength and how to fly,
To chase their dreams, to reach the sky.

With patience vast and wisdom deep,
To cradle them when they can't sleep.
To share in joy and soothe their fears,
Through all their days, through all their years.

A nurturing soul, a tender touch,
To give them roots, to love them much.
To show them grace and kindness true,
In all they say and all they do.

To be their guide, warm and bright,
To fill their days with love and light.
To be the mother I wish to be,
A harbor safe, a timeless sea.

In every moment, big or small,
To be their comfort, catch their fall.
To raise them strong, with hearts so free,
This is the mother I wish to be.

Finding Grace

In quiet moments, I feel a grace,
An unseen presence, a sacred place.
A guiding force, so pure and kind,
A gentle whisper in my mind.

Through trials faced and paths unknown,
I'm never lost, I'm not alone.
For in the shadows, light does gleam,
A divine hand, a tender dream.

God's love, an ever-present flow,
In every high and every low.
With every step, I feel the care,
Of God's embrace, always there.

Invisible, yet clear as day,
A loving guide, in every way.
I feel the touch, so soft, so near,
Of God's presence, calm and clear.

A force unseen yet deeply felt,
In every challenge, where I've knelt.
In prayers whispered, in tears shed,
In dreams that dance within my head.

So here I stand, with faith so strong,
With God beside, I can't go wrong.
In every breath, in every stride,
An invisible guide, forever by my side.

Aatishi

Aatishi, a name that speaks of light,
A dance of flames in the dark of night.
Dynamic sparks that pierce the sky,
Fiery trails where dreams can fly.

Aatishi, with power untold,
A heart of fire, fierce and bold.
Explosions of color, vivid and bright,
Shiny as stars in the darkest night.

With every step, the world ignites,
In vibrant hues and flashing lights.
Aatishi, a name that shines,
Through endless realms, countless times.

For in the heart where passions lie,
The sparks of my name will never die.
Born out of raging flames and might,
A symphony of fireworks, a soul's delight.

Alive in every stride,
Embers that burn with hunger so wide.
For in this name, a legacy resides.
Of courage, that never hides.

Through trials faced and battles won,
Spirit's soar, my journey has just begun.
Ardent, tenacious, in my quest,
A name that lives, forever blessed.